T0353834

A PhUN Day at School

Thomas B. deHaas Jr.

Illustrated by Heather deHaas

© 2024 Thomas B. deHaas Jr.. All rights reserved.

No part of this book may be reproduced, stored in a retrieval system, or transmitted
by any means without the written permission of the author.

Disclaimer
This book is fictional but based on real events experiences of the author as a student and teacher. The author struggled as a reader and spent 2 years in 4th grade. Both as a student and teacher, the author wants to encourage all students to find and follow their 'SPARK,' what makes them excited about life. By doing so, they can survive and thrive in school and life!

AuthorHouse™
1663 Liberty Drive
Bloomington, IN 47403
www.authorhouse.com
Phone: 833-262-8899

Because of the dynamic nature of the Internet, any web addresses or links contained in this book may have changed since publication and may no longer be valid. The views expressed in this work are solely those of the author and do not necessarily reflect the views of the publisher, and the publisher hereby disclaims any responsibility for them.

Any people depicted in stock imagery provided by Getty Images are models,
and such images are being used for illustrative purposes only.
Certain stock imagery © Getty Images.

This book is printed on acid-free paper.

ISBN: 979-8-8230-2476-1 (sc)
ISBN: 979-8-8230-2478-5 (hc)
ISBN: 979-8-8230-2477-8 (e)

Library of Congress Control Number: 2024907067

Print information available on the last page.

Published by AuthorHouse 04/25/2024

author HOUSE®

The author sincerely wants to thank his wife, Carole, who worked as an aide kindergarten through high school, his son, Thomas, who teaches middle school science and math, his daughter Heather (the illustrator), who teaches elementary art and is the school counselor. In addition, the author wishes to thank other teacher and staff from Mentor High School, Lake Catholic High School, Perry Middle School, and Perry Elementary School along with colleagues from The Ohio State University. Faith, family and friends made this book possible.

Waking Up

It was a warm spring night. I **rolled** out of bed. I wasn't going to **loaf**. It was going to be a phun day at school. I planned to **butter** up my teachers. I **rose** to my feet and **sliced** through the hall. I was thinking of **toast** for breakfast. I would have to **jam** it in, so I didn't miss the bus.

Breakfast

I decided to have **eggs** with my toast but had to **scramble** since the bus would arrive soon. The bus driver was here **eggsactly** the same time every day. I decided to eat only **the egg whites** because I had read, they were healthy, no **yolk**—for people, that is, not for the **chicken**. I added **orange juice** and **squeezed** it all in before the bus arrived. I was **peeling** full. I **scrambled** from the table and went to brush my teeth.

I wondered why it was called a **toothbrush**; everyone I knew had lots of **teeth**. Maybe the inventor was down in the **mouth** and decided to care for his or her last **tooth** before it fell out. I contemplated and was in deep thought about going to the **dentist** to have a **cavity** filled and how much the **Novocain** shot hurt; maybe I wouldn't get a **shot**. I'd just have to avoid the most painful time to go to the dentist, **Tooth-Hurty** (2:30). As I contemplated, the sound of the bus horn startled me.

The Bus Ride

It **jogged** my memory as I raced to grab my books and my lunch. I transferred them to my backpack and **sprinted** to the bus. I tried to sneak up the stairs, but all the kids were **timing** my arrival, which made me **stop** and **watch** my **steps**. I hurdled several book bags and finished just in **time**; I reached my seat and rested. I checked my own **watch**, which had **stopped**.

In **seconds**, I was seated next to my friend Matt, who asked lots of **questions** but had all the **answers**. The conversation went something like this:

Did you hear the one about the **rope**? .... It's too **long**. I'd have to explain it.

Did you hear the one about the **jump rope**? .... **Skip** it.

Did you hear the one about the **roof**? .... It's **over your head**.

Did you hear the one about the **hot coal?** ....I'd tell you, but I don't think you could **handle it.** Did you hear the one about the **construction project** .... I'm still **working on it.**

Did you hear the one about the **bed?** .... I haven't **made it up** yet.

Did you hear the one about the **broken pencil?** .... It had **no point.**

Did you hear the one about the **recliner?** .... It goes **way back.**

My head was **spinning** from all the jokes. Matt was on top of his game. As we **turned** the corner and **rounded** the **curve,** we **circled** the bus **loop** and came to a **rolling** stop.

As I unloaded from the bus, my mood was **lighter** from the jokes. I felt **uplifted** and **floated** down the stairs and walked **lightly** to my classroom. I felt the heavy steps of the principal behind me.

As students **streamed** into class, I had to **bank** on the idea it was going to be a good day, but something was **fishy**. I began to feel a little **clammy**, but the teacher **floated** into the classroom, and my fears subsided. I began to come out of my **shell**. I didn't want to be a **hermit** or let the other kids think I was **crabby**. It was going to be a phun day at school.

My First Class: English

In English class, we were studying **prepositions**. I climbed **aboard** my desk and got **about** my book, which was **above** my papers. I looked **across** the row to see if I was **before** or **after** my seat partner, who was **along** with me but **against** the clock. It was about the time to get started on the assignment at the teacher's signal. I didn't want to get **behind** because my grade might fall **below** an acceptable level, which would be **beneath** my expectations and put me **beside** and **between** my peers and not **beyond**. **But** by the time we started, I got **down** to my work. **During** the whole assignment, I knew all the prepositions except one. **For** the first time **from** the beginning in English class, I felt inside that I could see **into** the future.

It was **like** it was **near** to me and not **off** in the future, of course. I put my pen **on** my desk, **onto** the paper opposite my book. From **out** of the corner of my eye, I peered **outside** the window, **over** the trees, and **past** the playground **to** see a dog run down the sidewalk, since he got **through** the fence, to the gate, **toward** the school, **under** the swing set, and then **underneath** the slide. There he would wait **until** recess, come **up** to unsuspecting kids, and pounce **upon** them **with** all his weight **within** the play area, but **without** hurting them.

Finally, I concluded English class thinking of entering a **pun contest.** I would enter **ten puns**, but I had a feeling none of them would win. As it turned out, none of them won. Not **one pun in ten did.**

Math Class

Math class had always given me lots of **problems.** It seemed like the teacher had my **number** from the start and made me stand in **line.** But I don't want to get off on a **tangent.** I could count on the added stress, and my anxiety began to **multiply.** We were talking about **shapes,** and I felt like a math **seedling** that was growing up and eventually would say, "Gee, I'm a **tree (geometry)."** With **square** roots! The topic of the day was **circles.** As it turns out, **circumference** was not the largest knight at the **round** table, as I had thought. I assumed it was because he had eaten too much **pi.**

The problem at hand was about a **round Italian food** that was loved by kids and its volume. The problem went like this:

If **Z = the radius**, and **A = the depth**, what is the **volume** of this **round** Italian food?

I had a **slice** of insight that **cut** through my thoughts, and I blurted out, **"Pi zz a!"** to the **crusty** math teacher. She thought I was trying to be **cheesy** and put a dunce cap as a **topping** on my head and made me **bake** in the **hot**, sunny corner of the room. I was cut to **pieces** with humiliation, which the other kids **ate** up. I finished math class and was **full** of it. It was just one **problem** after another.

Social Studies

I always had **issues** in social studies. Today we were studying **maps**, which sounded like a **mountain** of fun. I could see a **path** to enjoyment as I **peaked** into the book. As I **crossed** the section on **rivers**, I was **flooded** with emotions but was able to **bridge** those feelings on my **road** to success. As we **traveled** through to sights and sounds, we saw **vistas** followed by dark **valleys**. It was hard to see the **forest** through the **trees**. My mind **wandered** for a time, thinking about lunch **dessert**. Or was it desert? There seemed to be a great range of **temperatures** in the class from **tropical** to **arctic**. The class had its **ups** and **downs**, but the **plane** truth was the time **streamed** along. By the end of class, I was ready to leave **atlas**.

Gym Class

I felt a little **clammy** when I arrived at gym class and was fearful of pulling a **muscle**. We were going to play basketball, which I thought was a little **fishy** to play in **schools**. It uses **nets**, and I thought **fish** who **swim** in **schools** stay **away** from the **nets**. The teacher was a **troll** and put us into a **line**. The captains picked teams, and the best players were trying to **lure** each captain to pick them. We were **baiting** each other, which was **reel** fun in itself.

The gym teacher told us we were playing **baseball**. We took the field **first**. **Second**, we chose a pitcher. **Third**, we took our positions. Our pitcher threw the **ball**, but then things began to go wrong. One of our players was **thrown out** for using **foul** language and another for **stealing** second. Another was **benched** for **striking** another player, who began to bawl so much he couldn't **bat** any eye. Fortunately, it began to **rain**, which **delayed** the game enough for us to **run home** to the school building. Overall, the experience was pretty **base**.

Lunch

It was time for lunch, and the menu said **pizza** and fries. It makes me think of **cheesy** jokes. As I passed through the serving line, the **crusty** old cook yelled, **"Cheese or pepperoni!"** When I got around to making the decision of which **slice** of goodness I wanted, all that was left was **cheese**. I took my tray and kept an eye on my fries. I grabbed a chocolate **milk**, which I **udderly** love, and some **carrot** sticks. I **rooted** around for ranch dressing and found some. I paid for lunch and went to the lunchroom.

The Lunchroom

I could feel as I entered the lunchroom some **main event** was about to happen. Then someone acted as the **ringleader**, and the food **fight** was on. It started with a box lunch first from the **right** and then the **left** of where I was sitting. Then someone spilled **punch**, and the lunch moderator grabbed a **fist** full of napkins. But it was not enough to **block** the barrage of food flying through the air. I **blocked** it from **hitting** me, and then the **bell sounded**. The principal stepped **into the ring** of leaders and took them **'round** the corner to her office. With that the food **fight** was over. Thankfully, no one got **knocked out**.

Science Class

My favorite class was science, and today we were going to study **outer space**. We began with **leaving earth**, which made sense to me, as I had just finished **launch**. We talked about **space explorers** and what they ate while in flight—**astro nuts**. We talked about preflight **training** and **preparation** and how they prepare—they **planet**. We talked about the **moon**. We discussed whether there was ever **life on the moon**.

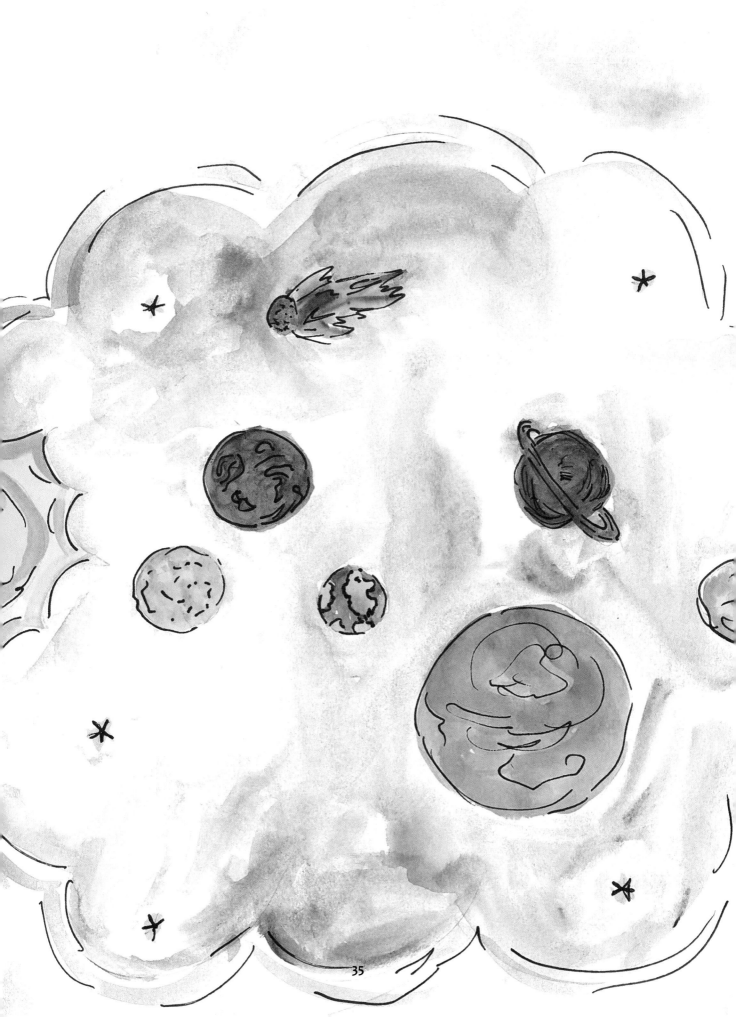

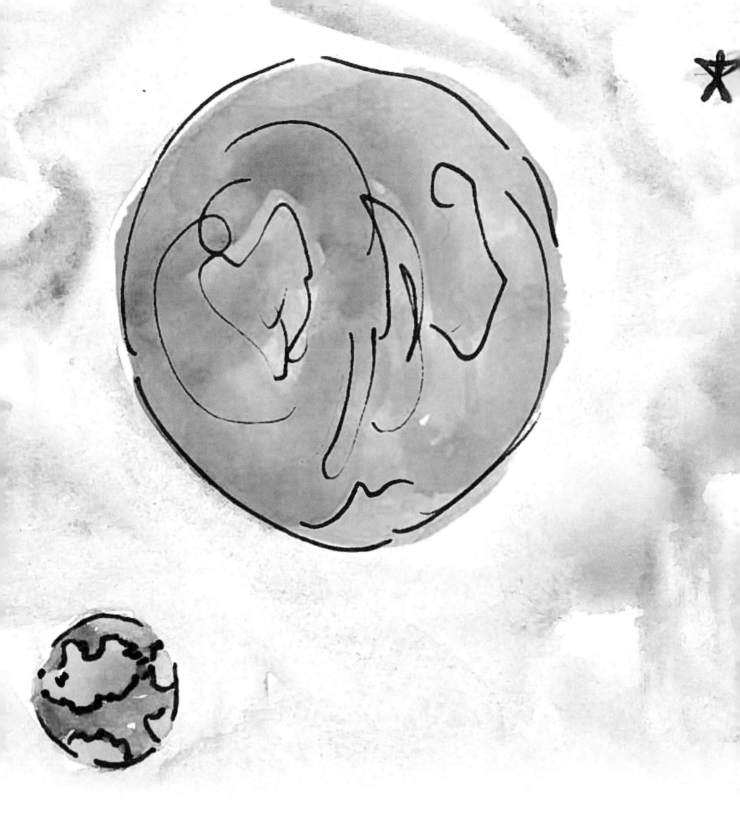

There was a theory that they found **bones** on the moon because the **cow** didn't make it. If someone **lived** on the **moon**, it would be kind of **cheesy**. If someone tried to open a **restaurant** on the moon, no one would want to come. There would just be **no atmosphere**. The whole discussion was out of this world. All of it made my head **spin**. I found my mind **drifting back** to earth when my teacher asked about **stars**. I told her I knew a lot about stars. In fact, my mom thought I was so **bright** that she called me **sunny**.

The teacher **launched** into a **ballistic attack** and **shuttled** me out of the class, and I would not **re-enter** until I spoke with the principal. This became my **mission** since she had **control**.

Talk with the Principal

My **mouth** usually gets me in trouble, so I was going to try to **keep it shut**. School would be coming to a **close**. I was **tight-lipped** when she began her **verbal** assault. Accusations flew, but I remained **silent**. When she stopped to take a breath, I smiled, which was the wrong thing to do. I was down in the **mouth** and **speechless** as she concluded her **tongue-lashing** and sent me back to class, instructing me to keep my **mouth closed. "Not a word!"** she said, which I found funny since she had **so much to say.**

Music Class

Today we would be singing in **music** class and learning about **notes** on the piano. My mom always told me to sing **solo**—so low she couldn't hear me. We began talking about **notes**. The first two notes were **C-sharp and B-flat**, which sounded like a clever idea for a joke. If you push a **piano** out a window or an elephant fell from the sky, you must **see sharp or be flat**. I told the teacher my joke, and she said, "Give it a **rest**." Then she showed us **A-flat minor**, which made me think of the poor miner at the bottom of a mine shaft with a **piano** on his head. I told the teacher, and she said my thoughts were **base**. I took a **note** of her **tone**, which was anything but **mono**.

She taught us that a piano has **eighty-eight keys,** which I thought would be handy for a **locksmith** to carry in his truck.

She showed us how to play **"Chopsticks,"** which just made me hungry for **Chinese food.**

The class was coming to an end, which was fine with me because it seemed to **repeat** itself. I was about to say something but decided to **refrain.** The **bell sounded,** which had a nice **ring** to it.

Study Hall

Study hall had two main purposes in my mind. Number one, entertain myself and number two, don't get in trouble. The problem was entertaining myself usually led to me getting in trouble. The **comedy** leads to **tragedy**, which creates **drama** for the bad **actor** who has chosen the **role** to **act** as a **character**. The climax comes when they are **cast** out of the room and **exit, stage left** to the **pit** in the principal's office. The principal will **orchestrate** a punishment that is anything but **music their ears**. As the **director**, she will not **play** with you but instead determines who will make the **final cut**, and rarely is it the **comic**.

I didn't try to make a **scene**, but the **script** had been **written**. It gave the **manager** on **stage** something that was anything but **music** to her ears. On my way to the principal's office, I thought of the **drama** that was **written** and realized I just needed to **play write**. When I arrived at the office, I remained quiet as a **mime** and went through the **motions** of listening. She sent me back to the hall to study, and the **scene** concluded as a **prelude** to my departure from the **theater**.

The Bus Ride Home

The bell rang, and the buses **rounded** the bus **loop**. My head was **spinning** from my **whirlwind** day, and I **bounced** down the sidewalk and **turned** up the stairs of the bus. I felt **deflated** as I **rolled** down the aisle. I wanted a nice, quiet ride home to prevent a tangle with someone else, so I sat **parallel** to my friend, who started giving me a **line** about how his teachers loved him and were **shaping** him into the next student council president to be above the other students. The conversation was **triangulated**, but it was the end of the **line** for me on a ride that seemed like **infinity**. At that point, the bus doors opened, and a **ray** of sunshine hit my face. I would soon be home.

Back Home

I was going to ride my **bike**, but was **two tired**, just like the bike, which was already laying down. I felt like a **fish** that had been in **schools** all day—actually, a **fish out of water**. I took a **deep** breath and **dove** on my bed. I had come out of my **shell** and felt like a **hermit**, which made me a little **crabby**.

I got up to get a snack, **cookies**, and **milk** because I was feeling a little **crumby** and didn't want to have a **cow** when my family came home, which would be **udderly** silly. I was on the fence. I went back to my room to lie down and close my eyes. I thought, It was a **phun** day at school. What about tomorrow?

The End!

(until tomorrow??)

Illustrator description:

Heather, the author's daughter, was a fine arts major at Ohio Wesleyan University. She concentrated in painting and drawing but enjoys creating mixed media art, including watercolors and ink. She is currently an elementary teacher focusing on school counseling and fine arts in grades K–2 in Ohio.